CONTENTS

OUR FRIENDS, THE SPIDERS?

What do you do when you see a spider? Most people jump away or at least back up slowly. Then, they think about whether to kill the spider or place it far away from them. Did you ever think about just leaving the spider alone?

Spiders are actually very useful to people. Of course, they don't know it, but just by living their lives, spiders help us. They eat insects, other **arachnids**, and small creatures, which helps keep some animal populations under control. Without spiders, we might be overrun by flies, mosquitoes, and other pests that are much more unpleasant to live with.

CREATURE CLUE

There are more than 43,000 species, or kinds, of spiders.

CREATURES
WE CAN'T LIVE
WITHOUT

We Need
SPIDERS

THERESE SHEA

PowerKiDS press.

New York

Published in 2016 by The Rosen Publishing Group, Inc.
29 East 21st Street, New York, NY 10010

First Edition

Editor: Caitie McAneney
Book Design: Mickey Harmon

Photo Credits: Cover (image) nico99/Shutterstock.com; cover, pp. 1, 3, 4, 6, 8, 11–13, 16–18, 22–24 (background) Click Bestsellers/Shutterstock.com; p. 5 MarkMirror/Shutterstock.com; p. 7 Joel Sartore/National Geographic/Getty Images; pp. 9, 16 Audrey Snider-Bell/Shutterstock.com; p. 10 basel101658/ Shutterstock.com; p. 13 (spitting spider) Stephen Dalton/Minden Pictures/Getty Images; p. 13 (jumping spider) skynetphoto/Shutterstock.com; p. 13 (bolus spider) Auscape/ Contributor/Universal Images Group/Getty Images; pp. 14–15 (main) Cathy Keifer/ Shutterstock.com; p. 14 (inset) Calvste/Shutterstock.com; p. 17 Sandra Caldwell/ Shutterstock.com; p. 19 Jorg Hackemann/Shutterstock.com; pp. 20–21 (main) symbiot/ Shutterstock.com; p. 21 (inset) Ainars Aunins/Shutterstock.com; p. 22 Hector Ruiz Villar/ Shutterstock.com.

Library of Congress Cataloging-in-Publication Data

Shea, Therese, author.
 We need spiders / Therese Shea.
    pages cm. — (Creatures we can't live without)
Includes bibliographical references and index.
ISBN 978-1-4994-0984-0 (pbk.)
ISBN 978-1-4994-1026-6 (6 pack)
ISBN 978-1-4994-1044-0 (library binding)
1. Spiders—Juvenile literature. I. Title. II. Series: Creatures we can't live without.
QL458.4.S535 2015
595.4'4—dc23
                                        2015012087

Manufactured in the United States of America

CPSIA Compliance Information: Batch #WS15PK: For Further Information contact Rosen Publishing, New York, New York at 1-800-237-9932

Spiders are helpful to us in some surprising ways. They've been on Earth longer than people—about 400 million years!

BUT THEY'RE CREEPY!

Perhaps so many people are afraid of spiders because of their appearance. They seem creepy because they look so different from creatures we think are cute and cuddly. Like other arachnids, spiders have eight legs and a body divided into two parts: the abdomen (stomach) and the cephalothorax (head and **torso**).

If that's not creepy enough, most spiders have eight eyes placed in rows on their head. Some have six or fewer eyes, though. Strangely, even with all these eyes, most spiders don't have good eyesight. They have different ways of catching **prey** than using their sense of sight.

CREATURE CLUE

Spiders are often called insects, but they're not. Insects have six legs, three main body parts, and feelers on their head.

This wolf spider has eight eyes, but some spiders that live in dark caves have no eyes!

WHAT ABOUT VENOMOUS SPIDERS?

Many people are scared of spiders because of their venom, or poison. However, very few species make venom that can harm people. The black widow, brown recluse, and Brazilian wandering spider are three spiders with venomous bites. Spider bites aren't usually deadly.

Scientists think spider venom could have important uses in **medicine**. Scientists at the University at Buffalo are studying how the venom of the Chilean rose tarantula might be able to treat muscular dystrophy. People with muscular dystrophy have muscles that get weaker over time until they stop working. Venom may be the answer to helping these people live longer and healthier lives.

CREATURE CLUE

Some scientists believe spider venom can be used for pain-killers.

The Chilean rose tarantula is a popular pet spider. It has hair all over its body.

Spiders usually live and hunt alone. Some use ballooning, or being carried by the wind while attached to a long piece of silk, to find new surroundings and more food.

SPIDERS WORLDWIDE

Some people think spiders are the most important insect predator, so it's a good thing they're found everywhere! Spiders are found on every **continent** in the world except Antarctica. Most live on land, but at least one species makes its home in water.

Many spider species prefer **tropical** areas to cooler areas. However, some spiders are found high in the mountains where it's very cold.

Tropical areas are home to many different kinds of bugs. We need spiders to eat these bugs, such as mosquitoes and flies, so their populations don't boom out of control.

CREATURE CLUE

The cane spider is found in many tropical regions of the world. It's responsible for eating many bugs in its warm, wet surroundings.

SMART HUNTERS

Scientists divide spiders into groups based on their hunting methods: those that actively hunt and those that build webs. Hunting spiders have good eyesight that they use to spot their prey. Jumping spiders leap great distances right onto their prey.

Web-building spiders usually don't see well. They build silk webs that trap prey and carry their **vibrations** to the spider. Orb weavers make a circular web that flying insects don't see until they're stuck in it. Bolas spiders let out one thread with a sticky drop at the end. They wait for prey to walk into it or even swing it at prey.

CREATURE CLUE

Trap-door spiders wait under the ground until they feel vibrations above. Then they attack!

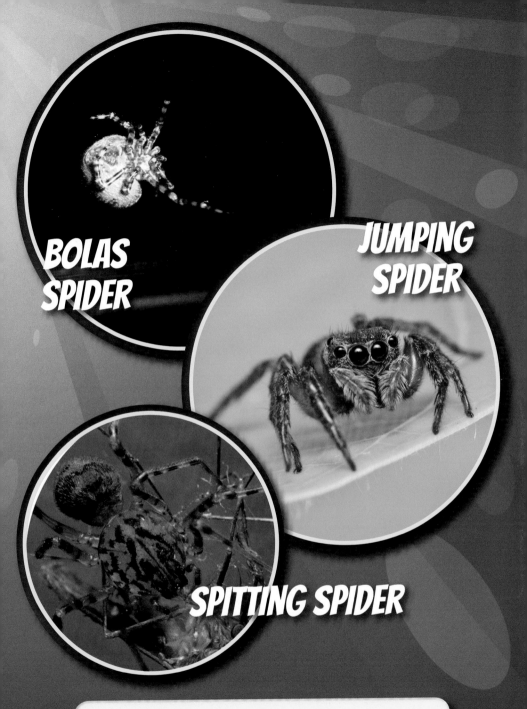

BOLAS SPIDER

JUMPING SPIDER

SPITTING SPIDER

Spitting spiders are hunting spiders. When they find prey, spitting spiders shoot a stream of sticky matter all over it.

13

SPINNERET

Web-making spiders use sticky and nonsticky silk in their webs. They know to walk on the nonsticky silk.

SUPERSTRONG SILK

A spider lets out silk from body parts called spinnerets. It wraps its prey in silk, turning the prey as it works. Then the spider may carry the prey somewhere until it's ready to eat. Most spiders make more than one kind of silk in their abdomen. They have different uses for different silk, such as wrapping their eggs and making a nest.

Spider silk is so strong that scientists are hoping it can be used someday to make bulletproof vests and strong ropes. Some companies are also trying to use it to make products such as shampoo and makeup.

CREATURE CLUE

Some scientists are studying spider silk for possible use in electronics. That's because spider silk allows electricity and heat to move through it.

SPIDER SNACKS

Spiders play an important part in their **ecosystem**. Ecosystems require a balance between the amount of animals and plants that live together. Predators must eat their natural prey to keep populations under control.

The Goliath bird-eating tarantula of South America is the largest spider in the world. It eats mice, snakes, bats, and sometimes even small birds. However, like most spiders, this huge arachnid mostly eats insects.

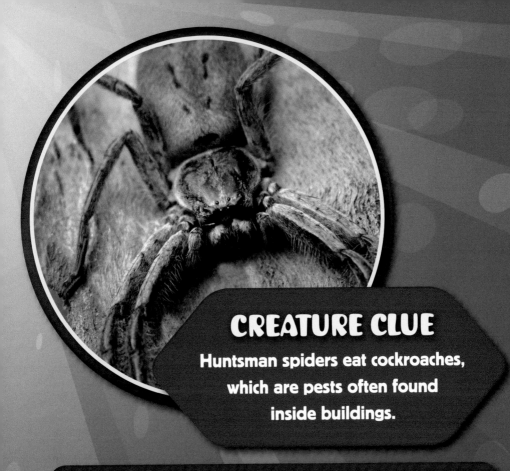

CREATURE CLUE

Huntsman spiders eat cockroaches, which are pests often found inside buildings.

Spiders help their ecosystems by eating many bugs and small animals. Some spiders are also food for other, larger animals. Depending on the species of spider, its prey can include crickets, flies, bees, grasshoppers, moths, butterflies, and other spiders. Some spiders hunt bigger prey. Six-spotted fishing spiders can walk on water and catch and eat fish. Some spiders can even catch fish five times heavier than themselves!

SEND IN THE SPIDERS!

Some scientists think pests would eat much of the world's food supply if spiders weren't around to eat them! More than 600 species of spiders make their homes on U.S. farms.

Spiders are such good predators that they've been taken to new locations to control insect populations there. They've been placed in apple orchards and rice fields to eat pests that ruin crops, such as grasshoppers. Many people think this is a better way to control pests than spraying crops with **insecticides**, some of which can harm people. Spiders are helpful for backyard gardens and inside your home, too.

A single spider eats about 2,000 insects a year. Would you rather have 2,000 insects in your home or one spider?

CREATURE CLUE

Spiders have been used to control pests in cotton fields in China, which helped reduce the use of insecticides.

HELP THE SPIDERS

Every time people cut down forests, clear fields, or change the natural world, they're **threatening** spider **habitats**. Some cave spiders, for example, are endangered, or in danger of dying out. Their homes have been flooded or even destroyed by people for building purposes.

Endangered spider species don't get as much attention as other species in danger. However, they're important, too. Not only do spiders help people by eating pests, spiders are an important food source for other animals, such as birds, lizards, and wasps.

Next time you want to squish a spider, remember all the good it does. Besides, it's scared of you, too!

CREATURE CLUE

Hummingbirds need spider silk to build their nests.

The great raft spider is an endangered spider species.

THEY KEEP ANIMAL POPULATIONS UNDER CONTROL.

THEIR VENOM MAY BE USED IN MEDICINE.

THEY EAT PESTS THAT HARM FOOD SUPPLIES.

WE NEED SPIDERS!

THEIR SILK IS USED BY OTHER ANIMALS.

THEY'RE A FOOD SOURCE FOR OTHER ANIMALS.

THEIR SILK MAY BE USED FOR BULLETPROOF VESTS.

GLOSSARY

arachnid: One of a large class of small animals that includes spiders, scorpions, ticks, daddy longlegs, and mites.

continent: One of Earth's seven great landmasses.

ecosystem: All the living things in an area.

habitat: The natural home for plants, animals, and other living things.

insecticide: Matter used to kill insects.

medicine: A drug taken to make a sick person well.

prey: An animal hunted by other animals for food.

threaten: To do something that is likely to cause harm to someone or something.

torso: The main part of an animal's body, not including the head, arms, or legs.

tropical: Hot and wet.

vibration: A small movement.

INDEX

WEBSITES

Due to the changing nature of Internet links, PowerKids Press has developed an online list of websites related to the subject of this book. This site is updated regularly. Please use this link to access the list: www.powerkidslinks.com/cwcl/spi